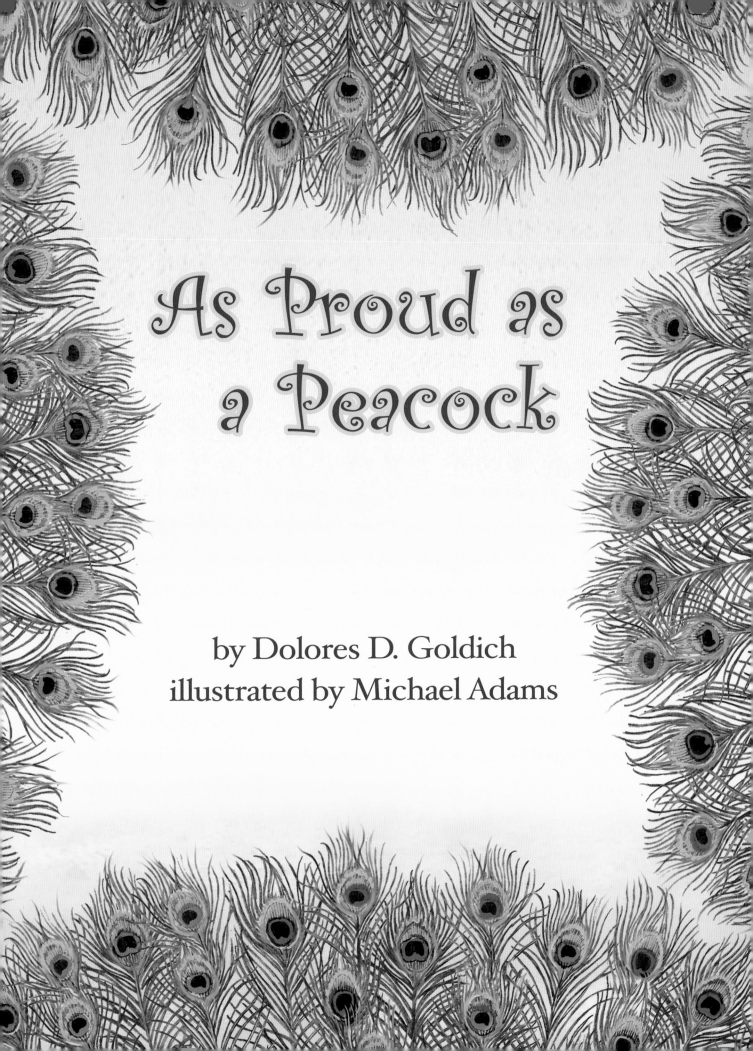

As Proud as a Peacock

by Dolores D. Goldich
illustrated by Michael Adams

To my precious children, grandchildren and sister
who are all beyond compare!
D.G.

For my granddaughter, Adilynn Grace Adams
M.A.

For further information, Contact the author at:
dgoldich42@comcast.net

Contact the illustrator at: michael-adams-studio.com
Book Design by Michael Adams

Dolores D. Goldich
As Proud as a Peacock
Summary: A Book of Animal Similes in Rhyme
[1. Animals–Fiction, 2. Children–Fiction.]
I. Adams, Michael. ill. II. Title.

ISBN: 978-0-9762915-1-0
Printed in the United States of America

Pavan just got a new puzzle;
He put each piece in place.
When the picture was all complete,
A smile was on his face.

Pavan was as PROUD as a ...

Peacock

Gabby wanted to make me laugh,
So she hid her face from me
By combing all her hair in front,
Where it's not supposed to be!

Gabby was as SILLY as a ...

Goose

Omar picked up a package
That was big and weighed a lot.
Mom said, "That weighs too much for you."
He replied, "No, it does not!"

Omar was as STRONG as an ...

Ox

Brianna wanted dinner;
She rushed to take her seat.
Whatever food was on her plate,
She could hardly wait to eat.

Brianna was as HUNGRY as a ...

Bear

Bruno played with his iPad,
Then read a picture book.
Later on, he played a game,
Then helped his daddy cook.

Bruno was as BUSY as a ....

Bee

Tessa was dressing herself for school,
And thought about what clothes to choose.
Which pants? Which top?
Old sneakers or new shoes?

Tessa was as SLOW as a ...

Turtle

Mason was told to brush his teeth;
It was very important - he knew it!
Unless his mom would stay with him,
He simply refused to do it.

Mason was as STUBBORN as a ...

Mule

Danita began a brand new school;
She didn't know what to say.
She found it hard to join the kids
When it was time to play.

Danita was as SHY as a ...

Deer

Luis got a puppy;
He treated it with care.
He held the puppy in his arms,
And stroked its soft, brown hair.

Luis was as GENTLE as a ...

Lamb

Mia's dad read her a story.
She wanted to hear every word
Because it was the scariest story
That she had ever heard.

Mia was as QUIET as a ...

Mouse

Chen woke up and smiled;
He is six years old today.
His friends will bring him birthday gifts,
And they'll eat and sing and play.

Chen was as HAPPY as a ...

Clam

Renata was drawing a picture
When she heard a banging sound.
She hurried to her sister
Whom she threw her arms around.

Renata was as SCARED as a ...

Rabbit

Owen liked to eat healthy foods
And get fresh air and exercise.
Another good habit he had was
Early to bed and early to rise.

Owen was as WISE as an ...

Owl

Lily went to the doctor
For a measles shot today.
She was very afraid of the needle,
But she stayed still anyway.

Lily was as BRAVE as a ...

Lion